Between 1733 and 1735 William Hogarth produced a series of paintings and engravings under the title of *A Rake's Progress*, which became perhaps his best known and most admired work. Motivated by Hogarth's example, David Solway tells the story of a representative figure, a lover, of our own anarchic era which is in some ways very similar to the dissolute and ostentatious period the painter anatomized. Solway has equipped the lover with a sketchy CV: he is an inveterate traveller – or perhaps 'cruiser' is a better word – and diarist with an introspective bent, but he is also a confirmed voluptuary prone to distraction and not without a streak of coarseness in his nature.

Images detailing critical moments in the lover's career have been contributed by internationally known artist Marion Wagschal.

Bathers

The Lover's Progress

POEMS, AFTER WILLIAM HOGARTH, BY

David Solway

IMAGES BY MARION WAGSCHAL

The Porcupine's Quill

NATIONAL LIBRARY OF CANADA CATALOGUING IN PUBLICATION DATA

Solway, David, 1941–
The lover's progress: poems after William Hogarth

ISBN 0-88984-229-9

I. Wagschal, Marion, 1943– . II. Title.

PS8537.04L68 2001 C811'.54 C2001-901873-8
PR9199.3S569L68 2001

Published by The Porcupine's Quill
68 Main Street, Erin, Ontario NOB ITO
www.sentex.net/~pql

Readied for press by John Metcalf; copy-edited by Doris Cowan.
Typeset in Bauer Bodoni, printed on Zephyr Antique laid,
and bound at The Porcupine's Quill Inc.

Represented in Canada by the Literary Press Group.
Trade orders are available from General Distribution Services.

We acknowledge the support of the Ontario Arts Council, and the Canada Council for the Arts for our publishing program. The financial support of the Government of Canada through the Book Publishing Industry Development Program is also gratefully acknowledged.

1 2 3 • 03 02 01

Canada

For Richard Wilbur

His drinking made him sick, his gaming made him poor, his mistresses made him unsound, and his other faults gave him some remorse.

Mary Davy, *The Accomplish'd Rake* (1727)

If what you have found was only a moment of light, like the explosion of a star, you would find nothing on your return.

Paulo Coelho, *The Alchemist* (1988)

Preface

> I have read your Play and find it will not doe.
>
> *A Rake's Progress*, Plate VII

I

Between 1733 and 1735 William Hogarth produced a series of paintings and engravings, under the title of *A Rake's Progress*, which became perhaps his best known and most admired work. In this sequence he told a story with which his time was already intimately familiar. A young parvenu, having inherited a fortune, resolves to emulate the stereotypical profligate and arranges his life according to the standard formula: make a young girl pregnant, buy her off, wench and gamble, be arrested for debt, marry a rich old harridan, throw it all away, proceed to debtors' prison, and end with tertiary syphilis in Bedlam. The pattern resembles a sordid and demonic Monopoly game predetermined by a near-invariable chain of Community Chest cards. When the dust settles we are left with a cautionary tale curiously neutralized, to some extent, by an extraordinary profusion of choreographic detail and an astonishing technical virtuosity, compelling delight and approval (or possibly resistance) in the aesthetic rather than the moral dimension. Not, I suspect, that Hogarth minded very much, however contrary to his avowed purpose.

Hogarth's intention in his large and crowded productions, as he put it in his *Autobiographical Notes*, was to 'compose pictures in canvas similar to representations on the stage.... My picture is my stage, and men and women are my players, who by means of certain actions and gestures, are to exhibit a dumb-show.' These dramas, as he explained some time later, derived from 'that intermediate species of subjects ... between the sublime and the grotesque', a form of representation that

Hogarth, alluding to Fielding's Preface to *Joseph Andrews*, called 'character', a vehicle for showing the crucial traits or features of his protagonist. (His congenial method was clearly understood by Swift who, in 'The Legion Club', playfully instructs 'humorous Hogart' to 'Draw them like, for I assure you,/You will need no *Car'catura.*') In order to render character as deftly, economically and resonantly as possible, he employed what he defined as a 'new way of proceeding, viz., painting and Engraving modern moral subjects' by arranging images into sequenced arrays which tell the story of a contemporary life so that, as Hazlitt shrewdly pointed out, there is a sense in which a Hogarth Progress has to be actively *read* rather than passively contemplated.

To facilitate this program, Hogarth devised a technical system of retention that permitted him to reduce both form and narrative to their basic elements, like his celebrated sketch of the serjeant with his pike and his dog entering an alehouse, rendered with only three strokes of the pen. Such economy was the fruit of what he called 'technical memory', a trained ability to observe rapidly and acutely, to retain 'in my mind lineally, such objects as best suited my purpose', to reduce his scenes at least initially to their constituent lines, and to represent the narrative development by framing selected incidents in a particular order whose links and continuities would have to be provided by the viewer. In effect, Hogarth proposed a kind of pictorial stenography that permitted him to record the essentials of his character's progress, abridging a complex and richly paradigmatic story into a frugal structure of revelatory moments. Thus, although the canvases and plates are teeming with life (mainly low life), the structural aspects of the development are spare and even parsimonious, requiring the participation of the viewer both to site the immediate circumstance and to infer the overall unfolding situation.

But after he had completed the engravings of *A Rake's*

Progress, deploying his protagonist's misadventures along eight successive instalments or plates, Hogarth was dissatisfied with the result and felt impelled to modify, revise, and intensify the octad through four additional 'States', furnishing new detail, adjusting balance and relation, and heightening or darkening his chiaroscuro. So as we follow Hogarth's own progress, we detect a gradual deepening of his theme, an obvious and cruder delight in censure giving way to a more serious and perhaps didactic judgement of the rake's decline and eventual degradation. It should be noted, however, that posterity has not always agreed with Hogarth's own estimate of his revisionary modulations, which would explain why the individual prints one finds in the various editions of this work are usually culled from all or most of the four States. For instance, of the eight plates reprinted in Ronald Paulson's authoritative volumes, the first six are Third State productions, the seventh derives from the Fourth State, and the eighth from the Second State.

2

Motivated by Hogarth's example, I also wanted to tell the story of a representative or emblematic figure of our own anarchic era, which is in some ways very similar to the dissolute and ostentatious period the painter anatomized, though of course very different as well. Like Hogarth, I wanted to present a certain 'character', neither sublime nor grotesque, who performs his drama on the contemporary stage; to select a series of telling gestures, actions, and reminiscences as adroitly and economically as I could; and to do so by contriving my own system of 'technical memory', projecting a suite of schematized events whose narrative structure would need to be supplied at least partially by the reader. (As Nietzsche said, 'with three anecdotes, it is possible to convey the image of a man.' To this end, I have provided a concise itinerary to suggest one plausible set of coordinates.) My intention was to transpose the Hogarthian precedent into a collection of poems corresponding to a procession of frames that record a 'modern moral subject': the state of love in a libidinous, self-referential, hedonic, and 'deregulated' age. But the social pretensions of the rake, who endures pleasure rather than enjoying it, who chooses fashion over passion and etiquette over companionship, would now be construed as the mingled preenings and lamentations of a modern lover for whom sensuality embodies a disabling belief in the impossibility of true intimacy. As Derek Jarrett remarks of the rake's vicissitudes, 'This is not a progress from one heady pleasure to the next but from one central delusion to the inevitable moment of disillusionment.' The same is true of the lover, but with this important qualification: the pursuit of pleasure has become the ironic correlate of *a contempt for the self* that is unequal to its longing for renunciation and fidelity (a theme, I might add, proleptically explored by Browning in a bizarre little poem called 'Porphyria's Lover' and afterwards developed by John Barth in a prose suite entitled *Chimera*). Another salient departure from the model involves the notion of the plural or equivocal subject; for example, it is not always clear who is speaking at any given time: the lover, the implied narrator, or the ventriloquial author. In such cases of address or attribution, it is the reader who must decide – or decide not to decide.

I regarded the lover as an exemplary figure (or collage) because he mediates in his typical assumptions about love, allegiance and reciprocity precisely the emotional and intellectual gradients of the age in which he lives. He conceives of intimacy as a kind of amphitheatre for the production of echoes and apprehends the 'other' principally as a stimulus for expression without commitment. His life takes on the quality of a periplus, a random navigation among islands that he inhabits only briefly and that, whether read as symbols for various states of mind, as place metaphors or as pleasure stations in a tourist archipelago, torment him with their evanescence. (It is mainly in Greece, naturally, that he finds mythological analogies and reverberations of his predicament.) And yet, despite – or maybe, in part, because of – his rhetoric and his epicurism, his acid suspicion that the self is inoperable, his refusal of all claims upon his concern, and his tendency never to be where he is but always somewhere else, in some imaginary or alternative world in which he figures as the axis of its rotation, a self-conscious mythic hero hankering for estellation, he retains a capacity to suffer flamboyantly, which does give him a certain dubious charm as it enables him at the same time to avoid the threat of total self-dissipation. As such he bears a partial resemblance to his illustrious ancestor, Edmond Jabés' Yukel, who, though always elsewhere, is at least sufficiently present to answer questions.

> 'What are you dreaming of?'
> 'The Land.'
> 'But you are on the land.'
> 'I am dreaming of the Land where I will be.'

In order to convey a flavour of the personal and avoid excessive generalization, I have equipped the lover with a sketchy CV: he is an inveterate traveller (or perhaps 'cruiser' is a better word) and diarist with an introspective bent, but he is also a confirmed voluptuary prone to distraction and not without a streak of coarseness in his nature, in other words, a dilettante, a professional amateur, a cultural sightseer who finds his niche in that genus of the modern that Max Weber foresaw and identified as 'sensualists without heart'. He suffers, as well, from the inability to reconcile wit and sentimentality that characterizes even the 'highest' of the type to which he belongs. I have made him not a wealthy *arriviste* like the rake but a member of the educated class who enjoys a reasonably independent lifestyle, speaks several languages, and has a taste for literary dabbling. But despite a sharp intelligence buttressed by a certain erudition, he is unable to resist the abundant temptations and seductions which life places in his path and which divert him from any long-term commitments he might from time to time consider. (The lover needs no Mephistophelean tempter as in the Auden-Kallman libretto of the Stravinsky opera: he is his own Nick Shadow.) Yet although he is not what some might regard as 'contemporary' in the sense of being electroliterate – he writes sonnets, after all, not code – he nevertheless remains in his nomadic and irresolute nature a reflection of the age he reflects upon, a man alienated even from his own alienations – from the *consciousness* of which condition he acquires whatever speculative authority he may be said to possess. (As Fielding commended in the celebrated Preface, such characters should 'appear to think'.) Only thus can he be both an astringent critic as well as a representative figure of the era that sustains him while simultaneously depriving him of substance and moral vigour.

3

With respect to my original model and in keeping with Hogarth's progressive darkening of his theme as a principle of development, I invoked the notion of successive States to suggest not merely the increasingly *penseroso* nature of my character's domestic melodrama but to chart his occasionally exotic itinerary from one place to another as he tries with a certain desperate insouciance to put his future behind him. These segments are also intended to map various states of being, related causally, each separated by a fall. The First State consists of what I might call hometown meditations, chronicling the lover's musings and encounters in his gradual descent into the darkness. The Second State, which opens with a journey abroad, comments on his growing awareness of his condition of exile, narcissism and loss. The Third State incorporates a miscellaneous travelogue that reflects the lover's mixed situation of panic and bitterness as he experiences the reality of his irreversible trajectory. And the Fourth State represents his entering into a condition of knowledge and rueful acceptance, a dark transparence in which he recognizes his basic and inwardly defining expatriate status and realizes that the fiery concomitants of a noble temperament are not his to absorb or display. This recognition and acceptance is the closest he can come to a sort of perverse heroism whose full consummation must necessarily elude his desire for reconciliation.

I have naturally taken some liberties in my interpretation of both the content and significance of each of Hogarth's eight plates, chiefly in the direction of interiority, replacing the conventional titles with my own in the process, although these latter do not appear in text but remain imaginary. Plate 1, 'The old home sold up', is reconfigured as 'Nostalgia', an easy enough transition to make. Plate 2, however, has undergone a sea change: where the rake is surrounded by artists, professors and parasites, I have had my protagonist encounter emblems of failure, whether in the world at large or in his own private and fabulary landscape. Plates 3, the 'Tavern scene', and 4, 'Arrested for debt', would now be retitled 'On the town' and 'In a state of arrest', respectively. Plate 5, 'Married to an old maid', *de rigueur* for the kind of progression Hogarth had in mind, is revised in accordance with the imperatives of the modern sensibility as 'Pursuing his affairs'. The sixth plate, the 'Gaming house scene', is diffused into a series of 'Gambling scenes', in which the lover is discovered wagering on romantic dereliction, like Frankie Laine's defiantly sentimental 'Moonlight Gambler'. Plate 7, the 'Prison house scene', transmutes inevitably into the condition of 'Imprisonment in the self', in which the chastened hero comes to the stark recognition of his internment within the unbreachable walls of temperament and habit. Finally, the eighth plate, the 'Madhouse scene', finds its counterpart in the lover's realization that, as a consequence of his many indulgences and his refusal to acknowledge limits to his Faustian desire for experience, he has condemned himself to his own inner Bedlam, a solitude paradoxically depicted as a kind of lucid delirium.

Thus the steps of a shadowy narrative progression, reprised four times in eight successive scenes whose differing circumstances bespeak modifications of inwardness, gradually come into view as the protagonist traces his journey from conjugal debacle through reverie, travel and various encounters with others (as well as with projections of the self and a cluster of symbolic objects) to a concluding state resembling something very close to solipsism, the manifestation of his potential condition when we first make his acquaintance. The lover and the rake emerge from the same inchoate process, move toward their different yet similar denouements, and perform their exemplary manoeuvres both in and on complementary stages, the social tableaux of the rake mirrored in the lover's psychic proscenium.

The Lover's Itinerary

First State

1. Leaves his wife. Sends, after subsequent reflection, regrets.
2. Meets a friend, in whom he sees a disturbing reflection of himself.
3. Goes to the disco. Remembers his Freud.
4. Hometown meditations.
5. Coffee with a potential mistress.
6. Discloses one reason for leaving his wife. Did he bet on the wrong woman?
7. Fears he may be trapped in his decision and that he has forfeited his wife's love.
8. A bad moment at the video arcade. Detects an appropriate metaphor of his condition.

Second State

1. Travels to Greece, where he visits 'the island'. Reads, translates, writes. Considers his state and intuits the nature of his dereliction.
2. On an excursion. Detects an appropriate metaphor of failure.
3. Goes to the movies. An quaint Indian film leads to reflection on the incommensurability between desire and fulfilment.
4. A day at the beach. His quest for sexual experiences and romantic preferment leave him exposed.
5. Covets a modern young woman, to whom he sends billets-doux, but is quickly timed out.
6. A debased Arion, he reflects upon his decision to travel, suspecting he may have lost his gamble.
7. Begins to understand the nature of his self-deception: false heroism and self-election.
8. A diving lesson at the Club. Detects an appropriate metaphor of his condition.

Third State

1. A hiatus. Having spent time elsewhere, he returns to the island. It becomes clear that he and his wife once lived there.
2. Sends her an inventory of significant objects that represent his failure both as a man and as a husband.
3. Has left the island and is now in Paris, where he goes to his favourite bar. His motives clarified, not without a sense of their absurdity, but also, perhaps, their necessity.
4. A homoerotic encounter. Reflects on Kierkegaard's family history. Realizes that in so ignoble and literally God-forsaken an age, love is devitalized by self-contempt.
5. Desires his wife again. Is it possible to return?
6. Is suicide an acceptable gamble?
7. Recognizes that he has hijacked his future.
8. Returns to the island. Metaphors of isolation, confided to his diary.

Fourth State

1. Realizes with renewed dismay the extent of his betrayal of the woman he continues to love.
2. Considers a variation of the myth of expulsion and return. More emblems of failure, which surround and occlude.
3. Goes to the café. Experiences a feverish carnival vision of the end of the world.
4. A tryst. Acknowledges the boredom of passion without love.
5. Recognizes that he is trapped in the erotic fabliau of his life. A hint of self-justification?
6. A moment of weakness. Calls his wife long distance, but understands he has lost the gamble.
7. Intuits that he can never arrive at (or return to) his true destination.
8. Accepts solitude. Knows that his life will always be touched by a sense of loss, that his future has passed him by, and that he is condemned to repetition.

Table of Contents

First State

... I'm howling 'youuu' through my pillow dike
many seas away that are milling nearer
with my limbs in the dark playing your double like
an insanity-stricken mirror ...

Joseph Brodsky, 'A Part of Speech'

The Bouquet

For the nights that I let bruise upon the ground
for the princess I betrayed with fairy tales
roses, roses

For the wine I spilled when I should have poured
for the friend whose pillow I have filled with thorns
roses, roses

For the bridges that I burned a second time
for the alphabet I cast into the wind
for the sabbath I abused with apricots
roses, roses

For the pot of basil I forgot upon the sill
for the tiny architecture of the Culver's root
abandoned to the weather of neglect
roses, roses

For the sonnets that I wrote but never sent
for reminding you without remembering myself
for the moon I sang no canticles beneath
roses, roses

For the salt I did not throw across my shoulder
for the orchard I delivered to the worm
for the flame that you kept cupped between your lips
and for the child whom I never bent to kiss
roses, roses

The Last Descartes

Don of the lower kingdoms, he
remains the philosophical
bachelor that he is. Surveys
his villa, his Honda, his girl,
and spoons his sherbet through the gaps
in his volubility, the
most inveterate of hams. Duchess,
sporting a corsage of new roses
'twixt matrimonial attempts,
is tied to his expressive wrist,
attends his dissertation, bobbing
the lovely yo-yo of her head.
No, he will not marry, will not
cede to Fate, pretender to his
throne, the dispensation of his
happiness. The last Descartes
of the nether realms, absolute
in his druthers, he understands
doubt is a way
of avoiding commitment.

At the Disco

Dig dat crazy gangsta
on de bongos, man.
Get dat beat, he say,
get dat beat, man.
Pounds dem bongos
like his mama's buns.
Dat jive honky on bass
he say, man
I don' need dis presshuh on
I don' need dis presshuh on
ME!
Life, man, life is duty free.
Hey babe, he say,
give Big Daddy a smackeroo.
Dat smoothy at de mike
he say, Down Rhona down
bring dat Suthun Comfoht ovah heah!
And dat uddah dude wit de beahd
he say:
a love that does not discriminate
forfeits all claims upon its object.

City of Lost Connections

At the Sunset Bar
you can get a BJ
for a whiskey soda.

In Hampstead
marriage is
the visible embodiment of
bad karma:
on the night table stand
the Kama Sutra and Kahlil Gibran.

On Crescent Street
the circular bed
and the mirror on the ceiling
reprieve the myth:
Narcissus resuscitated.

While beneath the Morning Star
on St. Lawrence Boulevard
rides the transvestite
in the back seat of the patrol car.

The Hostess

She brings him mocha coffee. Teas
of the finest blends appear
in jars upon her Chinese
tray. She leans above his ear.

At his feet the softest Greek
floccati to take the damp
away; underneath, pure teak
polished as a wishing lamp.

A premeditated lull:
a book is opened, shut; then
to perfect the ritual,
Brahms: direction, Karajan.

From the walls her quaint trouvailles
hang like trophies: a Moroccan drum,
gem-encrusted swords, a Thai
mask. Next, the aquarium

is remarked. Little tigers flex
intricate aggressive fins
as if in chase. She collects
ivories and porcelains.

The Oracle

'The wise prince makes decisive changes, new
succeeds upon the old.' Sweet Chinese.
'It is the barren womb that fructifies,
a lineage shall arise.' Good Hebrew.
'The warrior shall sacrifice the past,
his wound be his acquittal.' Sly Greek.
What was it the oracle meant to speak?
In choice of loves, next time you sit and cast

the coins, the yarrow stalks, the cards, the dice,
or ply your sortilege, beware of too
infatuate a trust in destiny
or fate. The oracle is mischievous.
Was it to leave the old love for the new
or yield the first her newfound mastery?

The Dream

I dreamt that you had ceased to love me,
not that you had come from other beds
back to mine, or gone from mine to others –
just something in your heart had simply stopped.

I willed myself awake to find you still
beside me. It was just a dream, I thought,
yet when I turned to kiss you, in your eyes
I saw that you had ceased to love me.

I willed myself awake a second time
to find myself alone, as I have been
these many months, but did not know if it
was terror or relief I felt, and whether

dreams unfold the past or make the future
plain. I dreamt that you had ceased to love me,
and know when I see nothing in your eyes
I can't will myself awake a third time.

The Arcade

Bells, the cash
        ching
in my cranial arcade.
Strobes freak, beep-tunes riot,
and painted doozies
                        flash
boobs on backboards
        as slavering aliens
        home their saucers in

                ping go the bumpers
                                flippers
flip right out
lasers hum,
        electric burrs
                stick in your ears
        skreeek   gurrrk

O solo mio
a whole fleet gone

And where is my princess now?

Second State

Survivors would have us believe in a brilliance
here, some bolt of truth forking across the water,
an ultimate Light before all the lights go out ...

Billy Collins, 'The Art of Drowning'

On the Island

With each line I cancel myself out
and my memory of who I was
and deliver my past in each unknown creature
that sees me walk by on the way.

I am my own messenger and come
from a land that does not exist
but rises before me as I gradually
forget that it lies behind me,

like a drunkenness that streams toward me
from things my coming gives shape to:
trees, rivers, pampas, winterly arrivals

in mountain villages and summer mornings at sea.
I have become the departure I never took
and have come to see what I once said.

– Translated from the Danish of Henrik Nordtbrand

[After translating this piece, he feels tired and depressed, and decides to walk to the little port some distance along the coast. There he translates the well-known 'To Limani' of Greek laureate Andreas Karavis, which is an earlier version of the Nordtbrand poem but in another register and idiom, since their situations are as different as they are the same.]

The Port

> Yet knowing how way leads on to way,
> I doubted if I should ever come back.
> Robert Frost

The dusty, untrodden road
I follow in the afternoon
takes me out of the intricate town
blurred with commerce and heat

and leads me to this airy cove's
white cottages and fishing boats
and the tall plane trees
munificent of shade.

The clean table puts forth fruit,
a jar of water, a paring knife.
I sit and stare at the sea,
pretending I am where I am –

Oh I know myself too well
to require less. I need you
as a man needs his consoling fiction
without which there is no returning.

Visiting the Caves

A party of tourists
with bouzouki as accompaniment.
They are ranged in two rows
along the side-benches of the bark,
chatting, doing crosswords, looking down
as if at their reflections in the sea,
waiting for the boatman.
They are off to visit the caves.
The bark sits high in the water
despite the many who have poured aboard.
They have taken off their sandals.
The boatman comes and unties the rope.
The boat glides past the lighthouse rock.
All symbolic as hell.

At the Movies

As the two heads move together,
the lips slowly approaching,
so slowly the distance seems to increase,
the audience slips to the edge of the abyss
between the screen and the pit.
The lips are nearly touching now,
betel and jackfruit, pomegranate and turmeric,
intimacy of red and orange,
now the lips are a membrane apart
eager to mingle spices
until, at the crux of tension,
a rose, a candle, a sunset
fills the screen
to the accompaniment of sitar and violin.
So now we must ask
what happened to the kiss?
Where did it go
before the lips touched,
after the intervention of beauty?
Or is it in the nature of kisses
never to occur,
to be cut from the mouth,
the consummation of failure,
blossom and flame and vermilion.

Sour Grapes

Cast up on the legendary coast,
shimmering in brine,
the mariner pretends to be asleep,

having furtively discarded his loincloth
to tempt the princess he is sure
will momentarily descend.

Day evaporates into night
but still she has not come.
He shifts uncomfortably on the stones.

And now he dreams her
soft and uvular moans,
her lips pouting like spoons

as she kneels where he fell.
At Ionian volutes of rock
broken on the shore

morning finds him bruised
and fruitlessly erect.
This is no way to treat a hero,

a subduer of demons and giants,
renowned for his deep subtlety.
He prepares to wait another day,

another night,
recalling his fabulous deeds.
And still she has not come.

The Bankrupt

With what can I purchase your attention
having no substance and no kind to spare?
Above us both the open-handed sun
flourishes his bankroll, a millionaire
to whom you offer all your pliant flesh.
How compete with the extravagant one?
By wit or beauty? I have no such cash.
By arrogance? By excess of passion?
I am in the shade, bereft of radiance,
so must wait my time like a mendicant
and bide your gradual indifference
in reaping in what still remains unspent.
I see you lounging on your balcony.
The light is like a coin upon your knee.

[Finding this poem ineffective,
he rewrites it in a more accessible mode.]

lover@nowhere.q.e.d

Never having mastered
the grammar of Indo-Nettian
or scrolled through contradictionaries
to find the right words
with which to impress
a power lady of your stamp,
I am bereft of the appropriate login,
I am not served in the chat cafés,
I receive no e-mail,
my dotcom has been discontinued,
the World Wide Web does not know me,

the screen mocks me with its radiant indifference.
O lovely neglectful madonna
I am lost for all of us.
Timed out before my time,
codeless in Cyberian dark,
I am benighted and alone
with none to heed
my corny antique eloquence
or the delicate charms of verse
that never failed me yet.

The Tourist

From the back of the Flying Dolphin,
Arion, with his slung Minolta
and heavy metal Walkman,
disembarks on the quay.

He has an eye for Swedish tits.
Who cares if this isn't Corinth?
Practising his lyric concordats,
ogles pussy on the cobbled plinth.

In Piraeus, ready to give up the ghost,
he was flung from the wharf.
Saved by the blue, emblematic beast
he skimmed the treacherous gulf

and found himself pitched widdershins
into the sticky honey of his lot.
He gathers up his travel things
and makes his way along the dappled port

to find accommodation. *Domatio,*
parakalo? Lathered in coconut oil,
Arion settles down to his espresso
marking out his share of loser's spoils.

Don Juan's Confession

I've made my bed with waywardness
and settled for a life
that brings me more of grief,
of gaunt despair and daily stress,

distress of mind and spirit-hurt
than virgin self-deceit
or celibate regret
could ever bring to break the heart.

Were it hatred of convention,
brave excess, urge to try
some new perversity
(for which one, later, might atone);

were it the unexampled art:
endeavouring to live
without ideals, to drive
the dreamer and his dream apart;

were it a life unreconciled
with time's consecutive,
through women to conceive
the eternity of the child,

or any laudable debate
with carnal diffidence,
reprieving by romance
a man who loved too soon too late,

I might persuade myself at last
  I suffered for all men –
  not for myself alone –
like your devout iconoclast.

The Diving Lesson

As you sink
images of women
float before the eye
like a shoal of red medusas
and at the bottom
an army of crustaceans
brandish their pincers.

You did not come
to hunt for coral
or to scour the seabed for treasure.
You came for tennis
and roulette.
You came to acquire a tan
with which to impress
your Charming Betty Careless.

Still, you think, the privileged
may be privileged,
as you wait to be rescued
from your rayless
element and reverie
by the pull of a former elegance:

glasses
tinkling across the supper table;
roses
on the dashboard of your Mercedes.

Third State

And to say trouth in wordes clere and playne
venereous people haue all theyr hole pleasaunce
theyre vyce to norysshe by this vnthryfty daunce

Sebastian Brandt, *The Ship of Fools*
(Translated by Alexander Barclay)

Revisiting the Island

The road leads him into many years ago.
There, in that white, spruced-up cottage,
Christine lay on her back and spread colossal thighs –
O fat she was, but with the face of a goddess.

(Up in the house on the spur of rock
above Kamini, a creature
known affectionately as 'The Wife'
poured wine and schemed her solitary revenge.)

And there on the left, the bakery's
crammed with sacks of flour
as it was when many years ago
the baker blanched white as his loaves

the time she asked for *psoli*
rather than *psomi*: penis
instead of bread. He recalls
her eyes were a heart-stopping green,

hair the yellow of lemon lilies,
and the cornflower-blue dress she wore.
(The house has gone as dowry now
to the crippled daughter with the swollen veins.)

And there, breaching the planes
of reminiscence, the blue hide of Whale Island
hoves up as he descends the cobbled steps
into the small port jammed with trawlers –

himself a caster of nets of – or out of – sorts,
hauling up nothing but debris, sea junk,
remnants, nothing for the skillet.
The fishermen, having gutted the catch,

are mending twine for tomorrow's expedition.
The coast road leading back to the town
trusses in the island's flaking shale,
binds it up and keeps it intact.

Here, at the halfway point, the Cavos Disco
jabs its strobes into darkened corners
lighting him into the present, the past, the present.
A vintage Wurlitzer plays the same old tunes.

The Gift

Here is the mandolin
my father did not teach me how to play.

Here is the genealogy
my mother slipped into my noblest dreams.

Here is the thimbleful of dust
I scraped in reverence from the poet's grave.

Here are the books
I also heaped upon the flames.

Here is the canopy of leaves
I crossed an ocean to drink wine beneath.

Here is the driftwood figurine
the sift of time turned copper-green for good.

Here is the cameo of the Baptist
who kept his distance out of self-esteem.

And, princess, here are the flowers
I was too much someone else to send.

At Harry's Bar

Sank Roo Doo Noo
I rakishly tell the driver.
There, with a little brandy,
a little companionship,
knowing the greatest distance of all
is that between two people,
I will make things clear.
I will send the world a fax
saying
the pleasures of infidelity
are meant to sweeten
the bitterness of subsequent remorse;
and the reason we cannot be alone
is that we are such poor company.
This accounts for everything.
I will then assure
the hostages of my appetite
they need never be afraid,
only offended,
at being held for such a modest ransom;
and that all I ever wanted
was a captive audience
to applaud the intemperate rite.
Oh if I could only strike it
emirate-rich and be respected
by my servants and dependents,
never needing to explain my reasons,
never needing to have any.
What joy!

I could just float above it all,
cool as Hugo Boss and bored as Faust,
or buy the Louvre and let it do
my serious remembering for me.
None of this is happening.
Everyone's broke and *unbehaust*,
little wampum left in wigwam.
Oh well, have another brandy, boy.

K's Papa

Only a god can save us now.
Martin Heidegger

When K's papa
cursed God in Jutland
The Sickness unto Death
was instantly conceived,
the fall of man re-enacted,
and a Baltic melancholy
diffusing its luetic grey
on all our works and days
immediately decreed;
also, the Quasimodo hump,
Regina out in the cold,
and an intense
susceptibility to caricature.

In short,
a general declination
to the void,
including the lapse
of the finer feelings,
leading us one by one
to suffer and magnify
on bended knee
the infirmity of the self
as we would
any other incurable disease.
Fact: in this world
we go down like fairies
on what we know
we don't deserve,
content with bitter electuaries.

Reconsiderations

O Serenissima
where are the grand old days?
Paparazzi springing out of the bushes?
Porfirio Rubirosa
and his red Ferrari?
The sweet sound of the ocarina
and the rosewood lute?
The *donna angelicata?*
The cultivated nuncios?
The count your master's known munificence?

It has to be one hundred percent
said the young historian
on the lookout for a wife.
His affair with the Estonian poetess
he assessed at ninety-one,
not quite enough.
Allowing for exaggeration, dear,
would you say … fifty?

Club Med

Tomorrow I'll pack up and go to Paradise
and there, among pelicans and fishingboats,
watch the beautiful people at their trades:
androgynes, glistening with sunscreen,
spreadeagled on the stones;
tanned young nymphs behind their visors,
mirror-lenses flashing like fish;
even bucket-laden serving maids
at their customary aspersions.

Tomorrow I'll pack up and go to Paradise
and there, between the biscuit bush and bongo tree,
give my nerves a long-needed rest.
I'll take a book with me, a pen, some paper,
or find some odalisque to pass the time.
It's easier than you think to shed your skin
once past the jet lag, as Epicurus tried to show,
between the airport and the dark casino.

The Hijacker

No hi-tech radical chic for him
no periscope light fixtures
no mellow globes floating in mid-air
no muted colonial splendours either
no sideboard with crystal decanters
no gentlemen adjourning for billiards
no Leucadian doilies on the liquor trolley
no red morocco guest-impressors
no wardrobe full of saffron suits
no English nanny for the young master
no pink Bentley for the sulking wife

a plank bed
a porcelain basin
a bare bulb

Fool!
All for a little power
a little pleasure

knowing
only the rich can afford to be poor.

Entries

• I could not stay indoors last night and went out to sleep on the beach, the ten thousand star hotel. The perpetual lapse of the waves at my ear, by receding, let the night fill up with the healing waters of reminiscence. No bad dreams for a change since this time I did not take the wrong abyss into the darkness. The gentle slope of the beach permitted an easy descent and, even more consoling, a gradual return with the lifeline of identity intact. But the day – that other night – is not kind to me. The strong wind and harsh sun strip me of directions. I dreamwalk past the white labyrinth of the town, finding no way in.

• At first I thought it was someone practising the recorder, a dedicated amateur repeating the same sequence of scales throughout the day and night with only short intervals of silence. Then, after about a week, I discovered it was the wind plucking a strange, medieval melody out of the telephone wires strung across the mountainside. At night, spotlit by the lime-cold glare of the moon, a solo cat picks its way beneath the wires and pauses, perplexed, to raise an answering cry.

• I walk along the shore of the wide bay and collect the shells swept in by the Libyan sea: glittering ormers, spiky murexes, tritons, helmets, wave-buffed cowries, spiral wentletraps, stippled moonshells, tiny dove shells and all kinds of rosy cockles and clams. The opercula of the knobby top shells, much valued by the people and called 'the eye of the sea', are set in silver and carried as talismans by lovers and fishermen on their various expeditions – which tend, on these islands, to be stormy. I send this inventory to her, this little door that opens inwards, set in a flange of white paper, bezelled margins of a lover's text. I live, now, inside this shell of words, rarely venturing into the real world, finding no way out.

Fourth State

And night doth nightly make grief's length seem stronger

Shakespeare, Sonnet 28

The Penitent

If you could see how much I miss you, dear;
if you could hear me now that we're apart
speak out my sudden fright, or rant like Lear
discovering too late his real heart,
and see the lion bewildered to the lamb;
or hear me in my unexpected need
recite some prudent, common epigram
to calm the heart and make its fear recede;
if you should add to this my sudden shame
that love could so reduce my dignity
I care for nothing but to hear your name
and care for no one who might comfort me,
you'd learn how I accept both shame and dread
because I know that each is merited.

The Reviewing

Sempre caro mi fu quest'ermo colle,
E questa siepe, che de tanta parte
Dell'ultimo orizzonte il guardo esclude.
Giacomo Leopardi

So might I, standing on this pleasant lea,
Have glimpses that would make me less forlorn …
William Wordsworth

But now, this time around, the view
I circled back here to enjoy
is different from the previous
year, its coffee on the terrace,
the chessboard over which we bent,
and *some* domestic argument.
The house was perched just high enough
to clear the fronting wall of roof
and hill and tree, and leave exposed
what, for others lower down, was closed.
The view then was as large as all
the islands of the heart were small
as if to compensate for lack,
the blue field of the sea so thick
with wave-bushes and wind-heather
you'd think anyone could walk there.

But now that I live without her,
settled in a little corner
at the bottom of the hill, a
tenant in a rented villa
communing with his glass of wine,

repenting for the pride of sin
by making sonnets that I send
like paper airplanes on the wind
(frail bulletins of love and rage
I ensure with double postage),
and know such limits once approved
by Leopardi, who had loved
(as Wordsworth loved 'this pleasant lea')
the hedge that hid immensity –
I see from my hedged-in terrace
a remnant-slope of splinter grass,
the islands levelled out with silt
and the merest shard of cobalt,
and curse, the view half-blocked by trees,
the inward infinite it frees.

The Apocalypse Café

Nick the waiter is balancing his tray
jittery with cocktails, as he
jaunts and cakewalks by the talking heads
swivelling on their pivots of bone
and waiting for a glass to fall. *Click.*
Someone takes a snapshot with a Polaroid.
A tiny engine grinds the picture out
which shows the future vast and empty
except for a tray hovering in the air
and three toy sentinels tall with swizzle-sticks.

Who is Nick the waiter? asks my girl.
(She is peering over my shoulder as I write.)
Just Nick, I say, just Nick,
not the devil or his surrogate,
a local boy hired for the season,
adept at whipping up the gorgeous
pink-and-lavender Malibu Specials –
one sip you're dead, another you're alive again –
that give this place its resonating name,
The Apocalypse Café, patronized by all.

Yes, but just the same, who *is* Nick the waiter?
asks another, invisible presence,
a woman, judging by the voice
and a doubt of fragrance clinging to the void.
Ask me another, I reply, and besides, who cares?
You'll find the boss more interesting,
Father Constantine, retired now, who speaks
a florid, liturgical Greek and a smattering of French,
an elegant gentleman soft in the head
who does *not*, be it known, stand for God.

Is he in the picture? asks my girl
(or is it the dummy perched on my knee,
with the shiny mumpish cheeks,
the barbed and mischievous temper I abhor –
I will stomp it to kindling on the café floor
very shortly).
No one's in the picture, I affirm,
neither Nick the waiter nor Father Constantine,
not you, not me, nor the perfumed absence
at the neighbouring table sipping her Malibu.

Now the tray comes hovering with another round
of Singapore Slings and salty Margaritas.
(The disco rhythms spoil my ventriloquism.)
The tourist flings his camera into the sea
which churns at the base of the postcard cliff
on which is poised the Apocalypse Café.
Nothing remains but the circling tray
which darts toward the window before it fades
along with the walls, the tables and chairs
and the startled clientele. Where's Nick? they ask.
    I reply, who cares?

Anagram

The question is: the ratio
of speech to prurience, candid
talk to kinky sex. Fellatio,
still, has much to recommend it.

Why gimble in the wabe? Buy all
her conversation up – or lack of
it – with praise of the labial.
Let her, at least, be active

in the art of consolation.
Yours, I mean. As for eloquence,
forget it. It's not her station.
Just let her nibble if she's tense.

The question is: how long will it
last, the brutal gag and cram
of mandarin roulette,
if boredom's bedroom's anagram?

Merlin on Nyneve

Half alive, I recline in stone
feeling my sinews blend and fuse
with the rock vein. The voices
I continue to hear in all
the tiny wind-hewn caves about
my dreaming head call me to take up
robe and emblem once again,
a summoning to the old
pragmatic uselessness
of policy and war. This trance
I once resisted with the strength
born of a saving cowardice
(arising not as legend tells
from spells and incantations
I once was master of but from
a sceptical, conservative
imagination) has merlined me
by inconceivable delights
into the stasis of desire
to unman me with my manhood.
I scarcely even resent this
bondage or condemn myself
for lassitude of will.
How could I deny
this bizarre emancipation
or bring myself to disavow
the exemptions of her beauty?

The Phantom

Phantom voices, urgent
and incomprehensible,
babble across the void
leaving their whisper tracks on tightropes
stretched between islands.

The dial spins like a roulette wheel.
Little balls of sound
click into niches,
till the croupier's voice speaks:
Monsieur, you have lost the connection.

I dial, hang up, dial again – hours; till
unbelievably it is you I hear
and I've forgotten what I wished to say.
My words stumble on their echoes.
You seem farther than before.

The Third Address

The first address is the easiest,
it comes to you eventually by itself
as you step into the taxi
and drive at breakneck speed
down the mazy streets of this familiar city
that has become strangely ominous,
the street-numbers rising like small moons
above the horizon of the windshield.

It is different, a little, with the second address.
Now you must stop at the fountain,
wander aimlessly while the driver waits,
the street names, the numbers
darting elusively in the shadows
like alley cats, like scraps of newspaper
blown in the wind,
like a scatter of clichés –
until, hours later, you have it
by the tail, the corner, the initial stroke.

The third address is another matter.
It escapes you forever,
it mocks you with its hidden presence,
it torments you with its evasive availability.
You have no choice
but to dismiss the taxi and awaken
if you are ever to find it again.
The third address is the necessary myth.
It is where you are never living.

The Insomniac's Lament

The nights grow longer when your sleep is short
and stars are staring through the window panes.
The moon is sailing to another port.

Whatever past it is your dreams distort
it's just a lunacy that never wanes
since nights grow longer when your sleep is short.

There was a girl once you used to court,
her love the kind all later love profanes:
now the moon is sailing to another port

and wind is coming from all sides to thwart
the indications of your weathervanes.
The nights grow longer when your sleep is short.

If heaven hangs on memory's report,
when paradise is lost, a part remains,
yet the moon is sailing to another port.

May as well tell the truth, the last resort:
the ghost you're working for is good with chains.
The nights grow longer when your sleep – in short,
the moon is sailing to another port.

Acknowledgements

A number of these poems, some in earlier versions, have appeared in *The Atlantic Monthly*, *The Canadian Forum*, *Canadian Literature* and *The Fiddlehead.*

I wish to thank the Conseil des Arts et des Lettres du Québec for a writing grant which enabled me to buy the time to work on this collection.

David Solway is the author of many books of poetry including the award-winning *Modern Marriage, Bedrock, Chess Pieces,* and *Saracen Island: The Poetry of Andreas Karavis.* His work has been anthologized in *The Penguin Book of Canadian Verse*, McClelland and Stewart's *New Canadian Poetry, Border Lines: Contemporary Poetry in English* from Copp Clark, and *The Bedford Introduction to Literature* from St. Martin's Press. Among his prose publications, *Education Lost* won the QSPELL Prize for Nonfiction and *Random Walks* was a finalist for *Le Grand Prix du Livre de Montréal.* His most recent prose work, *The Turtle Hypodermic of Sickenpods,* was released by McGill-Queens in 2001. Solway publishes regularly in such journals as *The Atlantic Monthly, The Sewanee Review, Books in Canada* and *Canadian Notes & Queries,* and is a frequent contributor to the Book Pages of the *National Post.* His more specialized writings have appeared in the *International Journal of Applied Semiotics, Policy Options: Institute on Research in Public Policy,* and the *Journal of Modern Greek Studies.* He was appointed poet-in-residence at Concordia University for 1999–2000.